I0150245

Dear Lover

The Human Side of Love

Elle Jay

Johnson Publications

Copyright

This book is a work of fiction. Names, characters, places and incidents either are products of the author's imagination or are used fictitiously. Any resemblance to actual events or locales or persons, living or deceased, is entirely coincidental.

ISBN: 978-0-9840416-9-5
Published by: Johnson Publications
Newtown Square PA

Copyright© 2016 by Johnson Publications
All rights reserved. No part of this book shall be reproduced or transmitted in any form or by any means without prior written permission of the author and publisher.

Cover layout/design by: Danny Denine Infinite Designs
Editors: Elle Jay
Typesetting: Rahiem J. Brooks

Printed in the United States of America

Contact for comments or to order books:
www.johnsonpublicationsbooks.com

Dedication

This book is dedicated to the one that gave me the inspiration to pick up the pen again and write from my soul. Muses come in all forms I will never forget the conversation and connection to this perfect stranger that opened me up to Love in many forms.

From the Author

The term Love is recognized in all languages. It is what most of us spend a lifetime seeking and some never have the pleasure of experiencing. In my experience Love is the one thing that gives me life and that zeal to Live and not Merely Exist. In creating this book, I wanted to express true love and not the kind that you find in the fairy tales. The truth is love has many layers and changes with the ticking of the timeclock. Love is a fascinating state of being, whether in full bloom or tainted with life circumstances, love is beautiful. Each poem or intimate writing will give you a bird's eye view as a voyeur in the beautifully flawed journey called Love.

Index

"**Love** is powerful. It can connect two souls and have them resemble one beautiful masterpiece."--
Elle Jay
xoxoxo

Falling Feels So Nice...

Many people get caught up in the feeling of falling in love. The experience of excitement and mystery of their new love quest keeps them engaged in the process and wanting more of the charge that love brings. The term falling in love is used because during this phase the body emits the same chemicals from the brain's pleasure zone as it does when free falling. The two lovers feel out of control and full of the pleasure hormone endorphins. This natural high is one of the greatest feelings. Truly connecting to another human being in that way awakens all senses and allows one to be present in each moment. If this phase is real and handled with care, you can fall in love daily as you discover something new about your lover that makes loving them that much more rewarding.

DEAR LOVER

Whisper

You got me going Baby
That thing you do to me that only you can
Got me wanting Baby, to be in your arms
Gaze into your eyes so we can give each other "soul food"
That feeling we get when we stare at one another with no
words... damn that's powerful
Sometimes I look away because our love is overwhelming
causing me to speak in a whisper
Wanting to say your name in between breaths just to have
you on my lips

I tell you how your love affects me because I need you to
know why I celebrate you every day

Although our love is built on more than our physical
connection
I can't help but to hunger for you
Wanting your lips on mine
Placed just right as our tongues dance in sync
Yearning to have your body adorning mine like my favorite
sexy dress...All over me!

Needing to have you whisper
That you love me
That you miss me

When I'm out of your presence
As I do the same

I love how we love each other
I can't get enough of the feeling I get when you give me what
I need
Filling every inch of me until I overflow giving you all of me
As I whisper how much you mean to me

The way I love you is different
Open
Honest
Transparent
I give you the most naked parts of me as we experience true
love

My mind is where I keep you close so that you are always in
my thoughts
My body is where you call home always warm inviting you in
My soul is where your anchored never to be removed

I will always speak and write about this great love of ours
When it becomes too powerful and my mortal body is weak
from time's grasp
I will whisper how much I adore you just so you never forget

DEAR LOVER

Blue Streaks

Electrifying, Magnetic is our attraction
In your presence I'm bound by our deep connection
You got me spellbound
Not wanting to come down from this high
Needing to be near you unable to control my reaction

You're my forbidden fruit dripping from my lips like sweet
nectar
Yearning for your touch to make it all better
Kisses so soft and sensual
Touch demanding and wanting
Our body language tells the story of us
Connected in a way that we can't control with words or
circumstance
Yet we get caught up in our own space
Both in a trance
Making plans
Asking what if?

Wishing that we could express this beautiful thing that just
happened
Sharing the joy we bring
But then we remember
This perfect dance cloud nine trance
Can't bleed out of the edges of the paper that holds our story
No matter how beautiful
This connection is confined within strict lines
With the harsh reality you are not mine
        Which leaves Blue streaks in my perfect skyline

Love Material

Thinking about you evokes emotions that I've never felt with another
You bring me the kind of joy that comes from within
Forcing its way out through smiles and that twinkle in my eyes
I can't help it

The love we share is commanding
Connecting us at the heart Strings
We love on the same frequency
You sense my emotional radar
Happy or sad and anything in between
You strive to fully dwell with me in any of these moments
Demonstrating that I'm not alone

I try to visualize how I thought and felt before you
I can't reach back that far
I feel as if I've loved you for a lifetime
As you let me see the reflection of your soul

You Fortify me
Loving me truly and obviously
Allowing me to feel how much you adore me with no words uttered

Thinking of you reminds me that somewhere in this world my love is known to its fullest potential and appreciated in its rawest form

Anticipation

I'm connected to you by an invisible string
Spanning miles across the land no matter how far apart
Quietly pulling my heart closer to yours

I try to occupy myself with life when we are not together
I always find myself
Anticipating
Wanting
Needing to be with you
Wondering how you are dealing with the space between us

I use the good memories that we create
Attempting to sustain me
Smiling as your image becomes so real I can reach out and
touch you
Forcing my mind to use its resources to comfort this yearning
inside of me

My mind with all of its vast knowledge is no match for the
love I have for you
Your love is undefeated
Winning every time
Making the anticipation grow stronger with each passing
moment

I anticipate hearing your voice to sooth my wanting
I anticipate your presence just so I can feel at home
I anticipate your touch that's so intense I feel all of your love
for me
I anticipate your love every day to make me feel whole

I know this colossal love appears impossible to survive
As I wrestle with this unwanted space between us
Seeking solace in my anticipation

Our love is so strong it forces me to transform
Pain into peace
Wanting into waiting
Anger into anticipation
Giving into my excitement of how wonderful our next
encounter will be
The way I'm going to hold you and kiss you
The way I'm going to Tell you how much I love you
As I declare that you're my true love and worth the wait

Falling 4 You

The floor dropped from under me
I began to levitate
Your presence reminds me that I am alive
Each one of my senses on high
The sound of your voice sends me falling, twirling over you
Yet I have no fear because I know I'm landing exactly
where I want to be
Your arms are home to me and your heart is my ultimate
destination
I'm stumbling
Falling heart first and you are there to catch me each time

Ordinary

My day consist of thoughts of you constantly
The moment my eyes open visions of your image invade my space

Some people may Say the love I have for you is unreal Too much

See they don't understand this thing goes deep because I recognize something special
So I protect and nurture it
As I watch it grow organically
Like untouched crops from the earth

This love ain't ordinary
Your love matches mine as you give me what matters most
That uncut sincere love and support
That thing money can't buy and time can't end

I carry you in my spirit everyday
Feeling your presence even when we are apart
Hoping for every area of your life to flourish

I replay our time together over and over just to be close to you
Making joy overflow from within like a bubbling brook

DEAR LOVER

I give you pieces of my soul
Declaring my Love for you constantly
Each time never the same
Day to day my love for you is fresh
Unique
Stronger
Making me have to tell you and show you in a new way
The words from 24hours prior are not enough
This love ain't ordinary

Love

"**There** is no greater compliment than a person

choosing to spend their time with you...when they

have so many other options. Time is special and

can't be recovered. Spend it with those that truly

love you and you them."--**Elle Jay**

xoxoxo

Love Connection...

Having someone that completes you is the most comforting feeling under the sun. The person that you look at and see your soul's mirror makes loving worth it. Having a connection with your soulmate provides you with a clear vision of your life's path and makes you want to live life out loud.

Dear Lover

Dear Lover I hope this letter finds you
I want you to know the level in which you touch my world
As my soul bleeds onto this page through pens ink
I'm sending myself to you in written form
This is my offering
You bring out a softness in me that I share only with you
Twirling and smiling as I catch the image of your face in mid-air
Placing my hand over my heart just to remind me of your home
Bringing me closer to you
When I found you I began to live
To breath so deeply that all cells in my body are aware
Caring for you so much
Each breath you take is important to me
Each heart beat counted as the rhythm of your pumping vessel becomes my rhythm also

You Touch my best parts hidden away like precious treasure
Your steady love brings these exquisite gems to the surface
You complete me
I am changed all because we took the chance to fall in deep as we tango love's dance
Never missing a beat
Remembering our special moments long after the song ends

DEAR LOVER

Dear Lover I hope this letter finds you
You must know that you are all that I can ever want
You arouse this quiet strength in me that provides
confidence in us
As I lean into you
Trusting and following your lead
I surrender my heart to you with no reservation
Lover you are the only one
Exclusively special to the love that I share
Without you I am inadequate
Lacking an essential part of me That's vital to my
survival
Dear Lover I hope this letter finds you and enters your
heart
Taking root in the secret parts reserved especially for me

Accountability

Accountability... A word that's used often but not fully
understood
By definition Means to be responsible for something

Accountability means much more to me
Owning your role is more like it
When you own something you claim it and protect it
I'm accountable to you
Fully accepting ownership for my part in your life
I don't take your love for granted
Nor do I give you mine halfheartedly
I am fully aware of how precious our love is
I am accountable to you
Giving you what you need
Making sure you always know the special place you hold in
my world

Your presence makes me feel completely safe and loved
Which makes being accountable to you easy
You make my smile bully its way from the Inside Out just at
the thought of you
You are such an important part of me
You are always in my plans
Constantly contemplating how my decisions will affect you

Loving you is my pleasure
Recognize I know how special I am to you too
You may not write me long love letters but you tell me every

DEAR LOVER

time we are together and I love that
The words you speak touches my soul and stays with me as a
piece of our history

Your touch lets me know you don't want to be far from me
The feelings are mutual
I don't know how or why we found each other
What I do know is more important
Loving you and being loved by you is amazing
You make life in this cold world worth the journey

Him

Your words touch me to the core leaving me
yearning for more of you

I know sometimes it seems as if I don't believe in the
amount in which you Love me

I just require more of you
More hugs and kisses
More I Love you
More I Miss you

This desire I have for you is insatiable
Don't be deceived by my need for more of you

I know you adore me

You love looking at me as your eyes tell the story

They say so much about how important I am to you

Your smile explains the joy that you have for me in
your heart that mere words do no justice

When we touch your love is transferred heart to
heart
The slightest contact with any part of my flesh
creates an exchange of physical chemistry
I can feel in my soul

DEAR LOVER

Remaining like ink stains on the pages of my heart
long after your touch has ceased

I'm part of your everyday thoughts

You look forward to sharing the most basic parts of
your thoughts and life with me as we laugh or even
cry about life's twist and turns

I recognize the depth of your love for me as you pull
me close to you
When we are together you are home
Loving just to share the same space with me
In silence or in deep conversation
For hours or just a few minutes

Your Love is evident ...crystal clear

My emotions affect you

You feel what I feel and take the time to show me
compassion in tough times
You rejoice with me in times of happiness

I fully understand how much you love me and what
I mean to you

I want you to know I feel your love and appreciate
you loving Me

Just Right

You're my get right
That glue that holds me together
Makes everything all better
The sight of you aligns the stars in my sight
Makes my world spin on its axis just right
You're my get right
Making my heart dance at the thought of your sensual glance
Forcing me to crave your embrace as my mouth reminisce on how good you taste
My get right
My get me right
Nothing is right without YOU

DEAR LOVER

Love On Repeat

Looked at our photo today
Reminiscing on a time when we were so happy
Our love was infectious to all those that lay eyes on us
I call it airborne love
So powerful it transformed something in Us
I truly saw you that day
I saw us standing in the sun as the rays exposed every corner
of Us
I was reminded how beautiful, powerful and scary love can
be
Just one look from you makes this uncertain journey worth it
I feel safe with you
Trusting this connection we can't quite explain
Knowing you love all of me
Like a favorite song this Love is on repeat
Everyday I awake
Same smile
Same feeling
Same craving
To love you more
Better than the day before
Wanting us to be more
So if either of us should leave
This feeling will last forever
Continually with our Love on repeat

Change

Something changed in me
It was like I saw you for the first time
I mean really saw YOU
You held my hand and opened your soul
I fell in deeper
Admiring the man you are from the inside out
Loving you more with every passing minute
Something changed that day
For the first time since our connection
We were at the same place at the same time
Loving in unison
Understanding Compassionate Patient love
Just when I thought my love for you filled me up
A deeper connection captured my heart
Causing me to overflow
Overjoy
Overdose on my favorite addiction YOU
You changed how I view things
I realized that loving completely and actually still exist
I'm forever transformed
I will never love the same again
Your love makes me want to
Be better
Do better
Giving you the best version of myself

"**True** Love makes us better in all areas of our lives. Loving the person, you were made to love aligns all things as they should be."--**Elle Jay**

xoxoxo

What Now

As I sit pondering the next time I will get to be close to you
I feel a deep pull in my core
Reminiscing on your touch
You have such an effect on me

Loving you is so rewarding
You appreciate how I love you and that makes me adore you
even more

I swore this would not be another poem
Just a long sweet hello
Mouth soft painted with a smile gave my voice a place to
escape
I spoke these words out loud

What Now?
As I thought... How else can I show and share my love?
Have I shown my deepest admiration for you?
Just as these words escaped my half parted lips my mind was
flooded with visions of you and so many more things I love
you for

DEAR LOVER

What Now?
You make me feel secure being loved by you
I know you love me sincerely wanting nothing but great
things for me
Even as we sit in silence your love for me changes the
atmosphere
Forcing me to share my vulnerability
Trusting you with my heart
The sight of you makes everything better
I love staring at you
It reminds me that I'm right where I want to be
Your eyes captivate me
As I look at you
You smile looking back at me
When my eyes sparkle that's only the reflection of what you
give to me
You care for and about me
Giving me genuine friendship
Listening to me as I bare my humanity
Taking special care of my fragile heart
As you provide me with sound advice to secure my future

What Now?
One hug from you satisfies me
Makes me whole
Your love is so rich and savory
Like a home cooked meal

Giving me nourishment that helps me grow
As a lover
As a friend
As a person
I love you for sharing yourself with me liberally and honestly
Leaving me caught up in your allure

All

You asked me for all of me
I paused as I contemplated the question
I felt naked just by your sincere desire to know every side of
me

I questioned the depths of my openness with you
How deep is too deep?
Should I allow you closer to me?

I give you my heart even the uncharted parts
My body is yours to please every desire as I open up to you
I am yours even though saying that out loud makes me aware
of the risk in loving
Even if I don't say it my heart aligns with yours
I sit in silence thinking about your request
I give in
I love you and trust you with my heart
Giving you me in the raw seems as natural as my love for you
So here is all of me
I'm yours for the taken
Request Granted

Dreaming

Who knew that my dreams that transpired in the past would
come true
So many years later
It's like subconsciously my soul knew what I needed
What I wanted was years away but I could not see that far
So I took a different course
As I toyed with fate

Today It's like I'm where I'm supposed to be
Our souls are a lock and key
Connecting
Bringing out that best in each other
Isn't that how love is supposed to be?
Isn't this how it's supposed to feel?
 Love should make you better
That's exactly what this love does for me
It makes me conscious of everything that should align
together
Loving you past even my own expectations
Placing your needs as top priority
Continually striving to meet them
Loving you is like déjà vu
Reminding me that my dreaming wasn't in vain

DEAR LOVER

This feeling is real
it's possible
I'm in it
Now the dream is reality
I find myself questioning how one person can make me
feel this extraordinary?
Then I realize that my doubt comes from years of loving
in a box
Believing the myth that time-in dictates the measure of
love

The manner in which we loved and were loved in the past
shapes our thinking
Makes us proceed with caution
Even though we know this love is epic
So I force myself to live in the now
I accept the bliss that we are in
As I embrace my reality that was once a dream
I'm no longer dreaming of you
I'm experiencing loving you
Receiving love from you and it's delightful

Satisfaction

As we travel through this thing called space and time we
don't always feel understood and supported
We often seek comfort and acceptance while searching for
unbridled love
I am so glad that you provide me with it all
Your love is so Rich & Filling
In your presence I'm not lacking or seeking
I am Satisfied

"True love never dies even during storms, it creates comfort and shelter for an aching heart."--
Elle Jay
Xoxoxo

Love On Pause...

Even the greatest of loves have their times when things are not always how they should be. Sometimes life's circumstances affect how love is shown or even if it can continue. I call this the human side of love. Sometimes wanting and needing or even missing. With all of loves changes the benefits always outweigh the problems. I can't imagine a world without knowing true Love, even if it's on pause.

Holding On

Today I missed you so much I replayed the last conversation
that we had in my mind just to have the sound of your voice
with me

Constantly my mind wonders
I find myself in captivity by memories of our encounters
A phone call, text or touch of your hand
Holds me hostage

I'm holding on to all that reminds me of you
Of Us
Clinging to our stolen moments just to be close to you

As time passes I realize that the distance between us draws
us closer
It forces us to think of each other often
cherishing every moment that we share
Not knowing the time or place we will be granted another
encounter
Makes me savor your presence

Not leaving a kind word unspoken
Your "I Love you" is sweeter and more sincere
Your "I Miss you" lingers long after our moments are over
I'm holding on to you
The thought of you and memories of us takes me to
uncharted territory in love where our love remains forever

DEAR LOVER

Space

I always carry you with me
No amount of space or time can change that
I know that we can't be together all the time
A day with no contact is incomplete
It's like I'm grabbing at air
Wanting a do-over
Wanting my time with you
With less space

Our time apart is hard
That does not stop this love from growing at a rapid pace
During this space between us there is an increase in the love
I have for you
 It allows me to reflect on our time together
Think about all of the things that make up us
I find myself smiling
Feeling real joy
As I recall how tender we love each other

I love you Baby in and out of this space we create
Your love urges me to color outside the lines
Expressing love without limits
I call your heart home and your arms paradise
    I look forward to the day when the space between us is
          minor and I'm back in your presence

Hello

Hello on the other end
I send out my love and sometimes I'm met with silence
The silence makes me pause
Evaluating my feelings
Not my love for you but my need to feel it from you

My love is guaranteed like 24 hours in each day
Given with a smile
Sweet and syrupy like apple pie
The taste is addictive

I give it to you because I have to demonstrate the bliss going
on inside of me
My love for you I can't hide even when I try
The thought of you makes my entire body smile

Hello on the other end
I send out my love
Sometimes it's met with silence... but I give anyway
The thought of you not experiencing my love for a day brings
me heartache

DEAR LOVER

As I imagine you not knowing that you are my true love
My soul's looking-glass
Reflecting what brings me happiness
So I share some more
I love sharing my love with you but sometimes the silence
makes me blue
   The only thing that can cure me is hearing and feeling love
from you

Love Remedy

As the days go on I wrestle with my feelings
As memories of us flood my mind constantly
A song on the radio
A simple phrase takes me right back to you
I press on as I try all that I know how just to feel whole again
How can I be whole when part of me sleeps with you at night
and roams your heart throughout the day
I'm working hard to settle into this new normal
Leaning close to my new life without you in it
I can't seem to get comfortable in this world of mine
No matter what I try
I trade Love for Lust that conveniently fall at my feet
Feels good for the moment with fleeting comfort
Hoping
Grasping
Trying to gather something just to fill this gaping hole in my
wounded heart

I whisper to myself "this is the right thing"
But my heart knows bullshit that my mind seems not to
recognize
The right thing is loving truly without limitation
So I accept that truth
Giving into loving you with all of my soul even in your

DEAR LOVER

absence

Time, space or location can't control Love and won't change
its power

No matter What

Thinking Out Loud

Do You Really know? How many times I plan to leave but can't let go?

I know it sounds crazy but Baaabbbby your love is That
Adam and Eve give me a rib so this thing can be complete
type of love

That bloodline to mankind
Like nothing can progress without you type of love

I tell myself daily just to close my eyes
Enjoy the ride
This enormous love I have for you I can't hide
Forcing me to share it so others can catch a glimpse of
something so real

The more I'm in your world ignites desires to be your only
girl
Making plans
Holding hands
Wanting that thing we do to each other

DEAR LOVER

Over and over again
While dealing with the reality of these invisible chains

Do you really know?
When I tell you I Love you I say it from my soul
No strings or hidden motives you just make me whole

Loving all of you
Mind
Body
Spirit
Soul
Understanding your story even the parts untold

I want you to know
I'm at war with my heart it's telling me it won't beat if we
ever part
It's saying
You're the one
This is it
So I surrender to it
I'm yours & you're mine
No matter what
This love is boundless
Won't even be contained by time

Reflections Of The Night

I stand in front of the mirror and take a deep breath
Admiring my reflection
Tonight is supposed to be special
I place my hair up in a sexy twist paying extra attention to
my makeup placement Being sure to stretch my long lashes
out enhancing my bright eyes
I pause and think...He loves my eyes and how I look at him
I see pain past these long lashes
I grab my body oil and proceed to rub it in slowly from my
ankles to my substantial thighs
I'm thinking about how good it feels to be touched by him
My mind wonders to the good times
Soul to soul times
I continue to prepare my body
I'm dressed
Looking like a Lady
Just enough sexy to keep the spark
I walk over to my full body mirror
Take a spin to be sure to admire all angles
leaning in close just stare at my image
As the mirror remains kind to me sending back a Pretty
Reflection
I give a half smile wanting so much to be as happy as I look
My heart quickens with loud heavy thumps
Sensing a heaviness in the depths of my soul

DEAR LOVER

Reminding me that this outside reflection is just Decorated Pain

Because the deep connection that brings me so much joy is forbidden pleasure

A reminder of my reality and what I yearn for daily

My awareness is heightened

Forcing reality to pierce through me like a sharp knife

I have a man in the next room excited

Waiting to meet this pretty reflection with a big smile

Take me out

Show me off to the world

My soul is at war

Torn

Attempting to look pretty even though my reflection would rather be with Him

The one that makes me beam with beauty from deep within my being as I truly experience euphoria

I quickly reset my thoughts to prepare to give this evening my all

I know the right thing but can't help how I love Him

How this love grows steadily leaving me wishing this night was with Him

Reflections tell a false story
My true reflection Uncertain and Broken
As All future reflections become shattered like fragments of broken glass
That even our love can't put back together

Absent

I miss your voice

I miss your stare

I miss your smile

I miss your smell

I miss your kiss

I miss your touch

I miss our witty banter

I reminisce over us

Reminding me how this hole got in my heart

Because you're not here

Devotional Love...

Sometimes in relationships people often talk about the spark being lost and things not being fresh. Well the fact is that love is a habit something that we have to practice demonstrating on a daily basis. In this section there is 23 love quotes to use to help you devote your love to your mate. You can use the daily quotes to send to your mate or use them simply as inspiration. The idea is to love each other actively on a daily basis. Letting each other know the special place held in each other's lives. Try it for 23 days and watch your connection become closer. It is one thing to believe in love but to practice it through gestures and words daily creates a closeness that is indescribable.

愛

Love

Habitual Love

I arise every morning with you in my spirit
As I think of how to demonstrate my love for you in a way
that is
Genuine
 Exclusive
Giving this special thing only to you
Love is a habit
A conscience effort demonstrating what you mean to me
I show you my love boldly and continually so that you get to
experience the euphoric feelings that you give to me
My eyes glisten with the reflection of our love mirroring my
soul's deepest emotions for you
You see it and feel how sincere my love is for you
As it transfers between us like uncontrolled electrical
currents
Love is a habit
Practiced in small gestures and intimate conversations as we
become so close our hearts blend into one
Relying on each other's survival
Love is a habit
Practiced daily
Given freely and never ceasing
Until I take my last breath and close my eyes I'll be Loving
You habitually

Love Quotes

Day 1:
My Love …You are rooted in the deepest part of my soul where only the best parts of me dwell. Loving you is necessary like the breath from my lungs.

_____
_____
_____
_____
_____

Day 2:
I thought of you today and my heart attempted to catch up with the speed that my Love grows for you. Grasping for air I realized this impossibility. My heart can't survive at that rate. See my love grows for you at the speed of sound and stays with me like my favorite melody that I play on repeat.

_____
_____
_____
_____
_____

Day 3:
Baby you give me something that can't be bought, borrowed or stolen. Each day this walk with you becomes sweeter. As we grow in love together it feels so great to love in unison. As we grow closer I receive more understanding of what true love is and why it's worth cherishing.

_____

_____

_____

_____

_____

Day 4:
Touching you is what I desire. Being close to you and feeling you is what brings me joy. It allows me to have a tangible experience with love. Touching, tasting and holding love in human form.

_____

_____

_____

_____

Day 5:
Baby you make my heart flutter. I love you so much. Each night I anticipate the morning excited to wake up and get 24 more hours of loving and being loved by you.

_____

_____

_____

_____

Day 6:
Baby you complete me! You enhance the way I experience life. Thank you for loving so well that I'm willing to open up my heart living and loving freely without restrictions.

DEAR LOVER

_____

_____

_____

_____

Day 7:
Never thought that our love would grow so deep. I'm scared to think about the depth of our love getting stronger as time passes. But excited about this good feeling. I'm glad to know that I have a friend for life that loves the entire Me.

_____

_____

_____

_____

Day 8:
I love you Baby 24 hours of each day. That is a guarantee. Everyday my eyes open I make an effort to share my love with you in such a way that no one else can and ever will.

_____

_____

_____

_____

Day 9:
As time lapse I feel all of the chains and restraints melt away... Loving you is like breathing... so easy and natural. You are a part of my existence and the role you play in my life is priceless.

_____

_____

———————————————————
———————————————————
———————————————————

Day 10:
If my pen was magic I would draw you close to me and write our love in history to inspire lovers for generations. I want everyone to experience something so beautiful that makes me want to live out loud and Something even rough times can't break.

———————————————————
———————————————————
———————————————————
———————————————————

Day 11:
I Love You 4ever... I just want to show you every day what loving you means to me. Every love story is beautiful... But ours is my favorite

———————————————————
———————————————————
———————————————————
———————————————————

Day 12:
My connection to you is made stronger with each hello... I fall in love with you in a different way daily as I learn to appreciate the person you are.

———————————————————
———————————————————

DEAR LOVER

_____

_____

_____

Day 13:
When I look at you I see the man that I love endlessly. I stare
a little longer and I'm captivated by your spirit. Always
sincere and compassionate which takes effort in this world. I
want you to know I see You and appreciate the man you give
me.

_____

_____

_____

_____

_____

Day 14:
Just when I think I've experienced everything your love does
to me... I feel a part of my heart that was tucked away just for
you to discover and make your own. Giving me more words
to share with you.

_____

_____

_____

_____

_____

Day 15:
Babe I have no regrets...You make my ♥ smile! If I had my life
to live over...You would still be my true love...But Next time I
would find you sooner so that I could love you longer.

_____

_____

_____

_____

_____

Day 16:
You give me hope... I cherish the love you give me because I know it comes from a place deep within that is not given easily. You inspire me with your quiet confidence and perseverance as you work through all that life throws at you. Through everything you never forget to Love me and for that you give me joy. Happy to call you my friend & my love. You may not have riches to give but what you provide is your heart and that's worth more to me than anything.

_____

_____

_____

_____

Day 17:
I'm holding on to hope... Each day I wish things were different, that our time together never ends. I'm so in love with you.

_____

_____

_____

_____

Day 18:
Love is the answer to all things. It's the only thing that can bind two hearts and make them so in tune that they beat the

same, feel the same and love the same. I am connected to you even when I don't try to be. Whatever part of the world you're in that's where my heart resides.

_____

_____

_____

_____

_____

Day 19:
I don't know when you became so important to me. It was like watching a rain storm. First you see a few raindrops and then a light drizzle... then it begins to pour and everything in sight is wet. You are my perfect storm and I'm flooded with loving you.

_____

_____

_____

_____

_____

Day 20:
I love you so much that if I had to choose loving you or breathing...I would use my last breath to tell you what you mean to me.

_____

_____

_____

_____

Day 21:
I wish that I could trade places with you so that you could see

yourself through my eyes and experience the joy that loving you brings me.

_____

_____

_____

_____

_____

Day 22:

Today I choose you. Loving you is my pleasure and being connected to you brings me peace.

_____

_____

_____

_____

_____

Day 23:

Life is worth living with you in it. Your love wraps me up and protects me. I love the way you love me... the way that you see me gives me energy that affects all that I come in contact with.

_____

_____

_____

_____

_____

DEAR LOVER

Love Notes:

_____
_____
_____
_____
_____
_____
_____
_____
_____
_____
_____
_____
_____
_____
_____
_____
_____
_____
_____

www.ingramcontent.com/pod-product-compliance
Lightning Source LLC
La Vergne TN
LVHW022136080426
835511LV00007B/1147